Sports Illustrated KID$

What Are The CHANCES?

The WILDEST PLAYS in Sports

Sports Illustrated Kids

Managing Editor Mark Bechtel
Creative Director Beth Power Bugler
Director of Photography Marguerite Schropp Lucarelli

Created by 10Ten Media

Managing Directors Bob Der, Scott Gramling, Ian Knowles
Creative Director Anthony Scerri
Writer Tim Gramling
Senior Designer Elizabeth Flach
Associate Editors Zachary Cohen, Nina Pantic
Reporter Corinne Cummings

Time Inc. Books

Publisher Margot Schupf
Associate Publisher Allison Devlin
Vice President, Finance Terri Lombardi
Executive Director, Marketing Services Carol Pittard
Executive Director, Business Development Suzanne Albert
Executive Publishing Director Megan Pearlman
Finance Director Kevin Harrington
Associate Director of Publicity Courtney Greenhalgh
Assistant General Counsel Andrew Goldberg
Assistant Director, Special Sales Ilene Schreider
Assistant Director, Production Susan Chodakiewicz
Senior Manager, Sales Marketing Danielle Costa
Senior Manager, Children's Category Marketing Amanda Lipnick
Associate Prepress Manager Alex Voznesenskiy
Associate Project Manager Hillary Leary

Editorial Director Stephen Koepp
Executive Editor, Children's Books Beth Sutinis
Art Director Gary Stewart
Director of Photography Christina Lieberman
Art Director, Children's Books Georgia Morrissey
Editorial Operations Director Jamie Roth Major
Senior Editor Alyssa Smith
Assistant Art Director Anne-Michelle Gallero
Copy Chief Rina Bander
Assistant Managing Editor Gina Scauzillo
Editorial Assistant Courtney Mifsud

Special thanks: Allyson Angle, Brad Beatson, Jeremy Biloon, Ian Chin, Rose Cirrincione, Pat Datta, Alison Foster, Joan L. Garrison, Erika Hawxhurst, Kristina Jutzi, David Kahn, Jean Kennedy, Seniqua Koger, Amy Mangus, Melissa Presti, Kate Roncinske, Babette Ross, Dave Rozzelle, Kelsey Smith, Larry Wicker

5,000

PASSING YARDS IN A SEASON

Only eight times has a quarterback thrown for 5,000 or more yards in an NFL season. The New Orleans Saints' Drew Brees has done it four of those times. No other quarterback has reached 5,000 passing yards in a season more than once.

CONTENTS

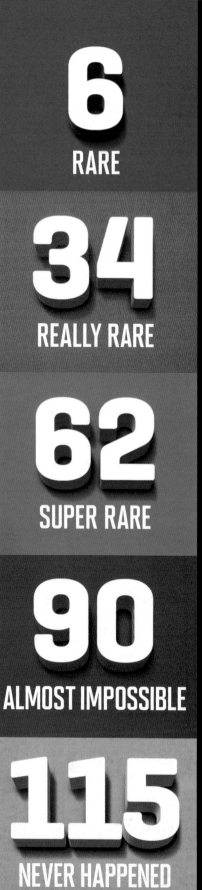
LeBron James of the Miami Heat had 32 points, 10 rebounds, and 11 assists in a 103–100 victory over the San Antonio Spurs in Game 6 of the 2013 NBA Finals. It was the 32nd time in league history that a player notched a triple-double in a Finals game.

RARE

Pittsburgh Steelers linebacker James Harrison returned an interception 100 yards on the final play of the first half against the Arizona Cardinals in Super Bowl XLIII. It's one of only 32 times between 1960 and 2013 that an NFL player returned an interception 100 or more yards for a score.

50

HOME RUNS IN A SEASON

When **Chris Davis** of the Baltimore Orioles led off the top of the eighth inning with a blast to centerfield against the Toronto Blue Jays on September 13, 2013, it was his 50th home run of the season. He hit it off All-Star reliever Steve Delabar and broke a 3–3 tie in a game the Orioles would go on to win, 5–3. It marked only the 43rd time that a major league player reached 50 or more home runs in a single season. Davis would end 2013 with 53 home runs, which was more than anyone in the majors.

5

TOUCHDOWN PASSES IN ONE GAME

An NFL quarterback had thrown five or more TD passes in a game 187 times through the end of the 2013 season. **Peyton Manning** of the Denver Broncos has done it eight times in his career, which is tied with New Orleans Saints QB Drew Brees for the most in NFL history.

Topps

JUNE 17, 1941

30
GAME NUMBER

Joe DiMaggio

NY

30
STRAIGHT GAMES WITH A HIT

★ JOE DIMAGGIO ★

Getting a hit in 30 straight games is rare — it's happened only 47 times in baseball history. The record for most consecutive games with at least one hit is 56, set by **Joe DiMaggio** of the New York Yankees in 1941. Only Pete Rose has reached 40 consecutive games since. Rose hit in 44 straight as a Cincinnati Red in 1978. Other than DiMaggio, no player in major league history has reached 45 in a row.

20
ASSISTS IN AN NBA GAME

An NBA player has dished out 20 or more assists in a game 227 times in league history, including the playoffs. L.A. Lakers legend **Magic Johnson** has the record for most 20-assist games in the postseason with 10. Johnson's single-game postseason record of 24 assists was set in Game 2 of the 1984 Western Conference Finals. It was matched four years later by John Stockton of the Utah Jazz.

4

STRIKEOUTS IN AN INNING

How can a pitcher strike out four batters in an inning when three outs are all he needs? If the catcher fails to field the ball cleanly on the third strike, the runner can reach first base safely if he's not tagged out. The strikeout is recorded, but not the out. Pitchers have struck out four batters in an inning a total of 66 times. It happened two different times in postseason history. Orval Overall of the Chicago Cubs did it against the Detroit Tigers in the first inning of Game 5 of the 1908 World Series. No pitcher struck out four batters in an inning in a postseason game again until 105 years later, when Detroit Tigers pitcher **Anibal Sanchez** struck out four Boston Red Sox batters in the bottom of the first inning of Game 1 of the 2013 American League Championship Series.

2 **HOME RUNS IN AN INNING**

In a game against the Houston Astros on July 26, 2013, Edwin Encarnacion of the Toronto Blue Jays became the 58th player in major league history to homer twice in the same inning. He opened the seventh with a solo shot and ended the scoring in the inning with a grand slam. He became the first Blue Jay to homer twice in the same inning since Joe Carter did it in 1993.

100 **YARDS ON INTERCEPTION RETURN**

There were 32 times between 1960 and 2013 that an NFL player returned an interception 100 or more yards for a touchdown. None of those interception returns came in a bigger spot than when Pittsburgh Steelers linebacker James Harrison picked off Arizona Cardinals quarterback Kurt Warner at the goal line on the final play of the first half of Super Bowl XLIII. His 100-yard return gave the Steelers a 17–7 lead in a game Pittsburgh would win, 27–23. It remains the longest scoring play in Super Bowl history.

TRIPLE-DOUBLES IN THE NBA FINALS

32

LeBron James tallied 32 points, 10 rebounds, and 11 assists in the Miami Heat's 103–100 win over the San Antonio Spurs in Game 6 of the 2013 NBA Finals. It was the 32nd time in league history that a player notched a triple-double in the Finals, and the fourth time James has done it. He and Magic Johnson are the only players with more than two Finals triple-doubles.

304

CYCLES IN BASEBALL HISTORY

A cycle in baseball occurs when one player hits a single, a double, a triple, and a home run in the same game. There were 304 cycles between when Curry Foley first accomplished the feat in 1882 for the Buffalo Bisons and Texas Rangers outfielder Alex Rios's cycle on September 23, 2013. Rios's cycle was the last of three cycles that occurred in Major League Baseball in 2013. **Mike Trout** of the Los Angeles Angels delivered the first cycle of that season. Trout became the youngest player in American League history — 21 years, 9 months, 16 days — to hit for the cycle. New York Giants outfielder Mel Ott, who is now in the Baseball Hall of Fame, is the youngest overall (age 20, in 1929).

10 BLOCKED SHOTS IN AN NBA GAME

A total of 43 different players have blocked 10 or more shots in a game. It has occurred a total of 154 times in NBA history. Utah Jazz center **Mark Eaton** accomplished the feat 19 times, which is more than anyone else in league history. Eaton, Hakeem Olajuwon and Andrew Bynum are the only players to block 10 or more shots in an NBA postseason game.

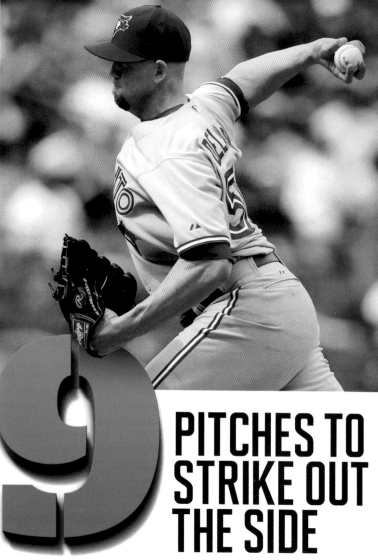

9 PITCHES TO STRIKE OUT THE SIDE

Relief pitcher Steve Delabar made history on July 30, 2013 by becoming the 47th major league pitcher — and first Toronto Blue Jay — to strike out three batters in an inning on just nine pitches. Delabar came on in relief of Mark Buehrle at the start of the eighth inning of Toronto's 5–0 victory over the Oakland A's and struck out Adam Rosales, Coco Crisp, and Chris Young. "It's pretty cool to do," Delabar said afterward. "I'm just looking to get in there and get guys out. To do it in nine pitches and strike them all out, that's crazy."

40

WINS IN A SEASON

Colorado Avalanche goaltender **Semyon Varlamov** saved all 31 shots he faced in a 4–0 victory over the St. Louis Blues on April 5, 2014. It was his 40th win of the 2013–14 season. Varlamov became the 47th goalie in NHL history to reach 40 wins in a season. Five days later, he notched his 41st win to break the team record that had been held by Varlamov's coach, Hall of Famer Patrick Roy.

113
HOME RUNS IN FIRST CAREER AT-BAT

Jurickson Profar of the Texas Rangers batted for the first time in the majors as a 19-year-old on September 2, 2012. He blasted a solo home run to right field off of the Cleveland Indians' Zach McAllister to become the 113th player ever to homer in his first major league at-bat.

6 HITS IN A NINE-INNING GAME

Alex Rios of the Chicago White Sox went 6-for-6 in an 11–4 win over the Detroit Tigers on July 9, 2013. He became the 32nd American League player ever to have six hits in a nine-inning game —no American Leaguer has ever hit safely seven times in a game that didn't go into extra innings. Rios also became the 69th player in either league since 1900 to get six or more hits in a nine-inning game. A total of five White Sox have accomplished the feat.

20 TOUCHDOWNS IN A SEASON

A total of 27 NFL players scored 20 or more touchdowns in a season through the end of 2013. The only player ever to reach 30 touchdowns in a season is running back LaDainian Tomlinson, who scored 31 TDs for the San Diego Chargers in 2006.

Ray Allen scored 51 points in Game 6 of a 2009 first round playoff series against the Chicago Bulls. He became the 33rd player ever to score 50 or more points in a postseason game.

50
POINTS IN A PLAYOFF GAME

28

HOME RUNS ON FIRST PITCH

When outfielder Starling Marte hit a home run on July 26, 2012, he became the 28th player in major league history — and first Pittsburgh Pirate in 51 years — to homer on the first pitch he faced in the majors. Marte's homer helped spark the Pirates to a 5–3 win over the Astros in Houston. "I figured he would take a strike just to see what I got," Astros pitcher Dallas Keuchel said after the game. "I never thought he would hit a home run on the first pitch of the game."

Steven Stamkos scored his 60th goal of 2011–12 in the Tampa Bay Lightning's final game of the regular season, on April 5, 2012. It was just the 39th time that a player had ever reached 60 goals in an NHL season. Stamkos received a loud ovation from the fans even though the game was played against the Jets in Winnipeg. "That made it even more special," Stamkos said afterward about the applause. "An ovation like that was amazing."

60
GOALS IN A SEASON

100

WINS IN A SEASON

The **Philadelphia Phillies** beat the Atlanta Braves, 4-2, on September 26, 2011, for the team's 100th win of the season. The Phillies became the 97th team in major league history to win 100 games in a season. They ended the season with baseball's best record, 102–60, but would go on to lose to the St. Louis Cardinals in the National League Divisional Series.

JOE MALONE

5 GOALS IN A GAME

★ ★ ★ JOE MALONE ★ ★ ★

A player has scored five or more goals in a game 60 times in NHL history. **Joe Malone** has the most career five-goal games with five. He did it for the Montreal Canadiens three times in 1917–18. He then had a seven-goal game and a six-goal game for the Quebec Bulldogs in 1920. Malone is the only player to score seven goals in a game.

277 NO-HITTERS

At the start of the 2014 season, a total of 277 no-hitters had been thrown in major league baseball history. Nolan Ryan set a record when he threw his fifth career no-hitter for the Houston Astros on September 26, 1981. Ryan went on to throw two more no-hitters.

6

TOUCHDOWN PASSES IN A GAME

A total of 40 quarterbacks have thrown six or more touchdown passes in an NFL game. When **Tom Brady** did it for the New England Patriots against the Tennessee Titans on October 18, 2009, he threw five of those TD passes in the second quarter. No other NFL quarterback has ever thrown five TD passes in a quarter.

10
SHUTOUTS IN A SEASON

Los Angeles Kings goaltender Jonathan Quick saved all 19 shots he faced in a 2–0 win over the Edmonton Oilers on April 2, 2012. It was Quick's 10th shutout of the season and marked the 53rd time that a goalie had reached double-digits in shutouts in an NHL season.

25

POWER PLAY GOALS IN A SEASON

A total of 29 players have scored 25 or more power play goals in an NHL season. Tim Kerr holds the record of 34, set in 1985–86.

30 STRIKEOUTS

There have been 64 times that a major league pitcher has struck out 300 or more batters in a season — six of those times were by Hall of Fame fireballer Randy Johnson . In 1999, Johnson reached 300 strikeouts in record time. He notched his 300th in only his 29th start of the season, on August 26, in the Arizona Diamondbacks' 12–2 win over the Florida Marlins. (The previous best was Pedro Martinez, who reached 300 in 31 starts for the Boston Red Sox in 1997.) "It's a special achievement," Johnson said afterward.

IN A SEASON

REALLY RARE

Miguel Cabrera of the Detroit Tigers became only the 16th major leaguer to win the Triple Crown when he accomplished the feat in 2012. Cabrera led the American League with a .330 batting average, 44 home runs, and 139 RBIs.

500

PASSING YARDS IN A GAME

Tony Romo of the Dallas Cowboys became the 15th quarterback in NFL history to pass for 500 or more yards in a single game when he threw for 506 against the Denver Broncos on October 6, 2013. Unfortunately for Romo and the Cowboys, superstar quarterback Peyton Manning was playing for the other side — Manning led Denver to a 51–48 victory to spoil Romo's effort. The 99 combined points made it the fourth-highest scoring game in NFL history.

10

RBIs IN A GAME

On August 21, 2007, Garret Anderson of the Los Angeles Angels became the 13th player in major league history to reach double-digits in RBIs in a single game. He drove in 10 in the Angels' 18–9 win over the New York Yankees. Anderson belted an RBI double, a two-run double, a three-run homer, and a grand slam.

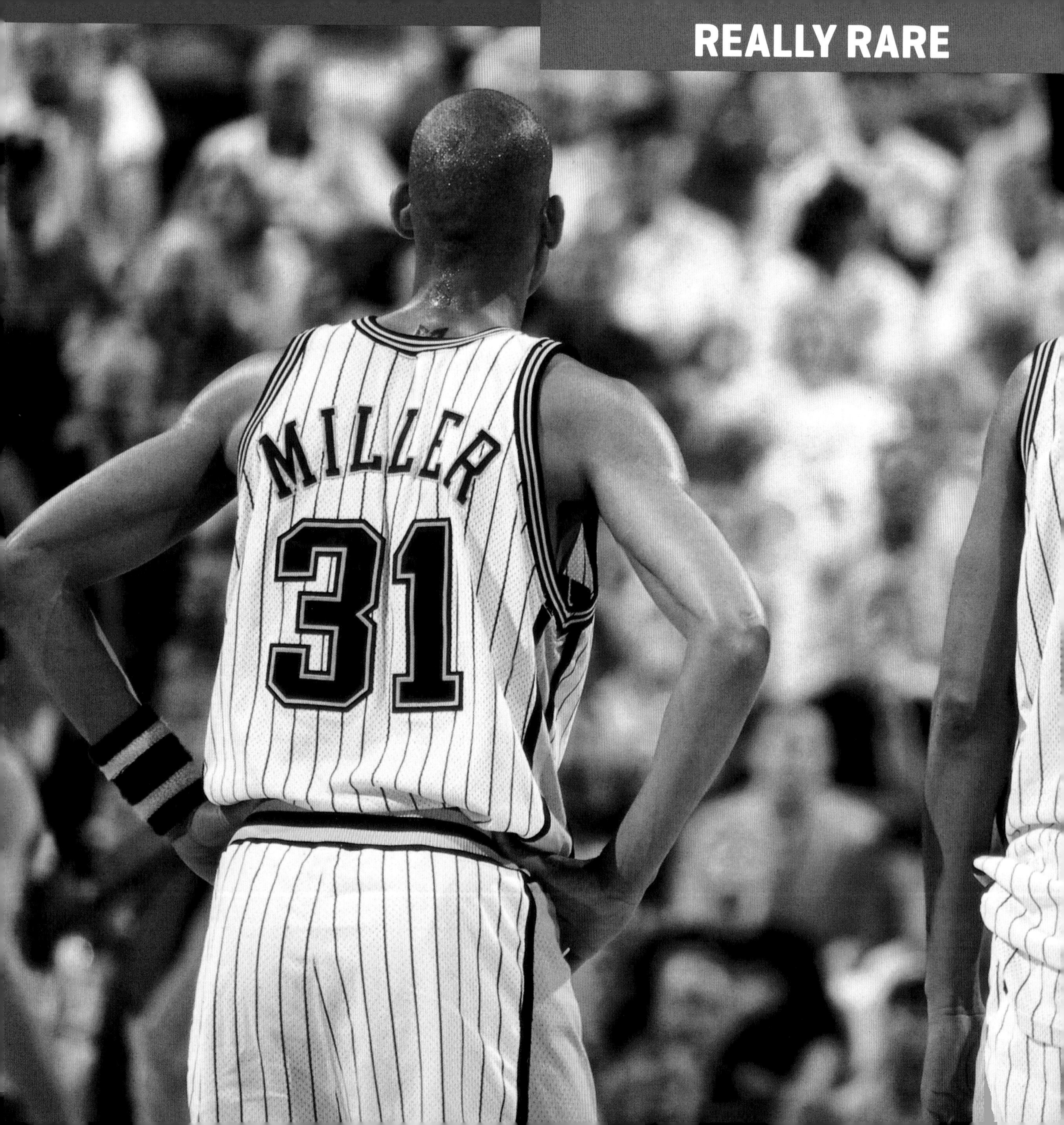
MILLER
31

40 POINTS EACH BY TEAMMATES

Teammates have each scored 40 or more points in the same game 14 times in NBA history. The last time it happened in a postseason game was when **Reggie Miller** and **Jalen Rose** of the Indiana Pacers each scored 40 in a 108–91 win over the Philadelphia 76ers in Game 1 of the 2000 Eastern Conference semifinals.

99

YARDS ON ONE PLAY

New York Giants wide receiver **Victor Cruz** scored on a 99-yard touchdown reception against the New York Jets on December 24, 2011. It was the 14th time in NFL history that a touchdown was scored on a 99-yard play from scrimmage.

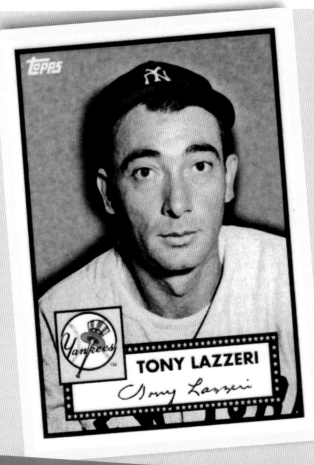

900

SCORE OVER THREE GAMES OF BOWLING

A 900 series is a set of three games with perfect scores of 300 each. On February 2, 1997, at Sun Valley Lanes in Lincoln, Nebraska, Jeremy Sonnenfeld bowled the first 900 series ever approved and recognized by the United States Bowling Congress. Only 22 other bowlers have accomplished the feat since.

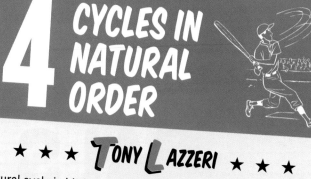

14 CYCLES IN NATURAL ORDER

★ ★ ★ TONY LAZZERI ★ ★ ★

A natural cycle is hitting a single, double, triple, and home run in that order, and only 14 players have ever done it. **Tony Lazzeri** became the only player to complete his natural cycle with a grand slam, in the Yankees' 20–13 win over the Philadelphia Athletics on June 3, 1932.

7

GOALS IN

O
A SEASON

Only 14 times has a player scored 70 or more goals in an NHL season. The last time it happened was in 1992–93, when both **Alexander Mogilny** of the Buffalo Sabres and Teemu Selanne of the Winnipeg Jets scored 76 goals.

10
STEALS IN A GAME

Only 22 times in NBA history has a player had 10 or more steals in a game. **Alvin Robertson** has the most career 10-steal games with four. The only other player with more than one career 10-steal game is Hall of Famer Clyde Drexler, who had two.

50

POINTS SCORED IN A SEASON

A total of 17 NFL teams have scored 500 or more points in a season. The only one to reach 600 points was the 2013 Denver Broncos, who ended the regular season with an NFL-record 603 points.

12

TEAMS RANKED NUMBER 1 FOR AN ENTIRE SEASON

The 1991–92 Duke Blue Devils were the last team to top the rankings for an entire men's hoops season.

16

TRIPLE CROWN WINNERS

Carl Yastrzemski of the Boston Red Sox won the 15th Triple Crown in major league history when he led the American League in batting average, home runs, and RBIs, in 1967. It would be 45 years until another member joined the club. Miguel Cabrera of the Detroit Tigers accomplished the feat in 2012 with a .330 batting average, 44 home runs and 139 RBIs.

100

ASSISTS IN A SEASON

When **Bobby Orr** of the Boston Bruins scored 139 points in 1970–71, it was the highest single-season point total ever by an NHL defenseman. He did it with 37 goals and 102 assists, becoming the first player ever to reach 100 assists in a season. A decade passed before another player reached 100 assists in a season: Wayne Gretzky of the Edmonton Oilers. Gretzky surpassed 100 assists in a season 11 times in his career. The only other 100-assist season in NHL history was by Mario Lemieux, who had 114 assists for the Pittsburgh Penguins in 1988–89.

23

PERFECT GAMES

The perfect game Felix Hernandez threw in the Seattle Mariners' 2–0 win over the Tampa Bay Rays on August 15, 2012, was the 23rd perfect game in major league history. Only one of those 23 was thrown in the postseason. Don Larsen retired all 27 Brooklyn Dodgers he faced in the New York Yankees' 2–0 win in Game 5 of the World Series, on October 8, 1956.

14

GOALS CREDITED TO GOALIES

In a game against the New Jersey Devils on March 21, 2013, Carolina Hurricanes center Jordan Staal tried to make a cross-ice pass during a delayed penalty after Carolina goalie Dan Ellis went to the bench for an extra attacker. But the puck hit off the boards, and went into the empty net for a Devils goal. Because **Martin Brodeur** was the last Devil to touch the puck, he was credited with a goal for the third time in his career, the most ever by a goaltender. A total of 14 goals have been credited to NHL goalies.

60

POINTS SCORED IN

A GAME

An NFL team has scored 60 or more points in a game 27 times, but only twice since 1990. The last team to do it prior to the start of the 2014 season was the New Orleans Saints. The Saints beat the Indianapolis Colts, 62–7, on October 23, 2011.

2 GRAND SLAMS IN A GAME

At the start of the 2014 season, there were 13 players who had hit two grand slams in a game. On April 23, 1999, Fernando Tatis of the St. Louis Cardinals became the only player to hit two in an inning.

40 COMPLETIONS IN A GAME

A total of 16 quarterbacks have completed 40 or more passes in an NFL game. The single-game record of 45 was set by New England Patriots quarterback **Drew Bledsoe** against the Minnesota Vikings, on November 13, 1995. Bledsoe had plenty to celebrate after his 45th completion settled into fullback Kevin Turner's arms in the end zone. The 14-yard pass gave the Patriots a 26–20 overtime victory and capped a stunning comeback from a 20–0 deficit after Bledsoe had completed only eight passes during the first half.

UNASSISTED TRIPLE PLAY

BILL WAMBSGANSS
CLEVELAND INDIANS – 2ND BASE 10/10/20

15 UNASSISTED TRIPLE PLAYS

★ ★ ★ **BILL WAMBSGANSS** ★ ★ ★

Only 15 players have turned unassisted triple plays. The only one to do it in a World Series was the Cleveland Indians' **Bill Wambsganss**, in 1920. In the fifth inning of Game 5 against the Brooklyn Dodgers (then called the Robins), he caught a line drive, stepped on second base to retire a runner, and tagged a runner who had been on first base.

16

DOUBLE EAGLES IN A MAJOR

Louis Oosthuizen took his second shot with a 4-iron from the middle of the fairway on the par-5 second hole at Augusta National during the final round of the 2012 Masters. He hit the ball 253 yards, between two sand bunkers, and watched it roll across the green, from left to right, and into the hole. It was the fourth time in Masters history and 16th time in a major golf tournament that a player holed out for a double eagle, which is a score of three strokes under par. The other three double eagles at the Masters were by Gene Sarazen in 1935, Bruce Devlin in 1967, and Jeff Maggert in 1994.

21

NO-HITTERS THROWN BY ROOKIES

In only his second major league start, on September 1, 2007, Clay Buchholz of the Boston Red Sox threw a no-hitter in a 10–0 win against the Baltimore Orioles. It was the 21st no-hitter ever thrown by a rookie, and the second time that a rookie threw a no-hitter in his second major league start (Wilson Alvarez of the Chicago White Sox threw a no-hitter in his second start, on August 11, 1991, also against the Orioles). The only rookie to throw a no-hitter in his first start in the majors was Bobo Holloman of the St. Louis Browns, on May 6, 1953.

12

COLLEGE BASKETBALL UNDEFEATED SEASONS

There have been 12 times that a men's college basketball team has finished a season without a loss. John Wooden coached four UCLA teams to perfect records, in 1964, '67, '72, and '73.

22

HAIL MARY TOUCHDOWNS

With 8 seconds left in the fourth quarter and his Seattle Seahawks trailing 12–7, quarterback **Russell Wilson** took what would turn out to be the final snap of a game against the Green Bay Packers on September 24, 2012. Wilson rolled left and threw a Hail Mary pass into the end zone toward wide receiver Golden Tate, who was in a crowd of three defenders. Both Tate and Packers safety M. D. Jennings got their hands on the ball, but officials ruled it to be a complete pass, resulting in a Seahawks' game-winning touchdown. It is believed there have been 22 Hail Mary touchdown passes since Dallas Cowboys quarterback Roger Staubach popularized the term after his 50-yard game-winning pass against the Minnesota Vikings in the 1975 playoffs.

27 NHL TEAMS HAVE COME BACK FROM A 3-TO-1 DEFICIT

When the New York Rangers came back to beat the Pittsburgh Penguins in the second round of the 2014 Stanley Cup playoffs, it marked only the 27th time in 273 series that an NHL team won a best-of-seven series after trailing 3–1. The only Number 8 seed to come back from a 3–1 series deficit to beat a Number 1 seed in the Stanley Cup playoffs was the Montreal Canadiens in 2010. Goalie Jaroslav Halak saved 41 shots in a 2–1 Game 7 victory over the Washington Capitals, who had the NHL's best record during the 2009–10 regular season.

60 POINTS IN A COLLEGE BASKETBALL GAME

Only 25 times in Division I men's basketball history has a player scored 60 points in a game. The record for most career games of 60 or more points is held by LSU's Pete Maravich, who accomplished the feat four times. The first time Maravich did it was during his junior season, when he scored 66 points against Tulane on February 10, 1969. He surpassed 60 points three times as a senior in 1969–70, scoring 61 against Vanderbilt, 69 against Alabama, and 64 against Kentucky.

6

CONSECUTIVE GAMES WITH A HOME RUN

Only 17 major league players have hit home runs in six or more consecutive games. Three of those players share the record for most consecutive games with a home run, with eight. The most recent player to homer in eight straight games was Seattle Mariners outfielder Ken Griffey Jr., who did so in 1993 from July 20 to July 28.

10

THREE-POINTERS IN A GAME

J.R. Smith of the New York Knicks went 10-for-22 from beyond the three-point arc in a game against the Miami Heat on April 6, 2014. It was only the 20th time that a player made 10 or more three-pointers in a game, and Smith's 22 three-point attempts were the most ever in one game. The record for most three-pointers made in a game is 12. It was set on January 7, 2003, when Kobe Bryant of the Los Angeles Lakers made a dozen three-point shots against the Seattle SuperSonics. Donyell Marshall of the Toronto Raptors matched Bryant's feat on March 13, 2005, when he came off the bench to hit 12 three-pointers in a game against the Philadelphia 76ers.

SUPER RARE

When Chicago Bulls legend Michael Jordan scored 3,041 points in 1986–87, it was only the fourth time in NBA history that a player scored 3,000 or more in a season.

10

COMBINED NO-HITTERS

On June 8, 2012, Seattle Mariners pitchers (pictured, from left to right) Kevin Millwood, Charlie Furbush, Stephen Pryor, Lucas Luetge, Brandon League, and Tom Wilhelmsen combined to no-hit the Los Angeles Dodgers. It was the 10th time in major league history that two or more pitchers combined to throw a no-hitter.

ROUND OF 59

Annika Sorenstam became the first LPGA golfer ever to shoot a round of 59 when she did it with 13 birdies in the second round of the 2001 Standard Register Ping. While Sorenstam remains the only woman to shoot under 60 in an LPGA tournament, Jim Furyk became the sixth PGA golfer to shoot 59, in the 2013 BMW Championship's second round. Furyk made 11 birdies to go along with an eagle on the par-4 15th hole.

KICKOFF RETURNS FOR TOUCHDOWNS IN THE SAME GAME

When Leon Washington of the Seattle Seahawks returned two kickoffs for scores in a game against the San Diego Chargers on September 26, 2010, he became the 10th player in NFL history to accomplish the feat. His first touchdown was on a 101-yard return at the start of the third quarter — it was the longest kickoff return ever by a Seahawk. Washington nearly had a second third-quarter kick return for a score, but he was tripped up by the Chargers' kicker near midfield. He got another chance, after San Diego tied the game, 20–20, with 6:39 remaining in the fourth quarter. Washington received the kickoff at his 1-yard line, then raced 99 yards for the game-winning score in Seattle's 27–20 victory.

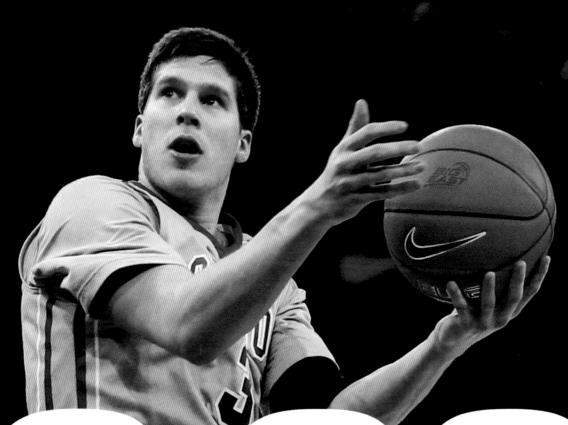

Midway through the second half of the Creighton Blue Jays' 88–73 win over Providence on March 8, 2014, **Doug McDermott** hit a long jumper to become only the eighth player in Division I men's college basketball history to reach 3,000 career points. "I saw on the Jumbotron that I was two away," McDermott said afterward. "So I just gave it a shot, got a good look at it, and it happened to fall."

3,000
POINTS IN A COLLEGE CAREER

8

COMEBACKS FROM A 3-TO-1 NBA PLAYOFF SERIES DEFICIT

The Phoenix Suns became only the eighth NBA team ever to come back from a 3–1 deficit to win a seven-game playoff series when they did so against the Los Angeles Lakers in the first round in 2006. After winning Game 5 easily, 114–97, to cut the series deficit to 3–2, the Suns won Game 6 in overtime, 126–118, behind 32 points and 13 assists from star point guard **Steve Nash**. Phoenix returned home for a 121–90 victory over Los Angeles in Game 7. The Suns jumped out to a 17-point lead in the first quarter and never looked back, shooting a blistering 61 percent from the floor.

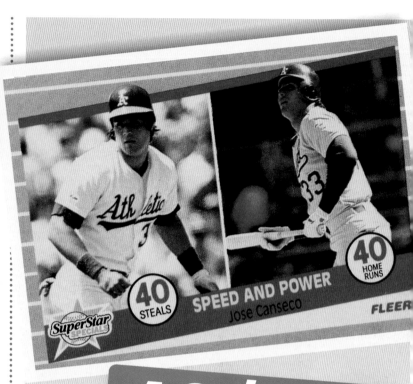

SPEED AND POWER
Jose Canseco

1,000

CAREER ASSISTS IN COLLEGE

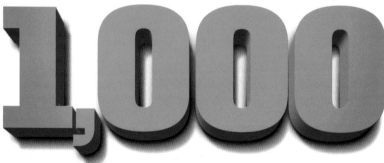

Going into the final game of his career at Long Island University on March 1, 2014, Jason Brickman needed three assists to become only the fourth player in NCAA Division I history to reach 1,000 for his career. He got 12 to join Duke's Bobby Hurley, North Carolina State's Chris Corchiani, and North Carolina's Ed Cota in the 1,000-assist club.

40/40 CLUB

★ JOSE CANSECO ★

Only four players have ever stolen 40 or more bases while hitting 40 or more home runs in a major league season. The first player to do it was **Jose Canseco**, who had 42 homers and 40 steals for the Oakland A's in 1988. The 40/40 club's other members are Barry Bonds (1996), Alex Rodriguez ('98), and Alfonso Soriano (2006).

4

COMEBACKS FROM DOWN TWO SETS IN A MAJOR

Only four times between 1968 and 2013 did a player come back to win after being down two sets in a best-of-five Major tennis final. **Andre Agassi** accomplished the feat against Andrei Medvedev at the 1999 French Open.

PASSING YARDS IN A SEASON

Only eight times has a quarterback thrown for 5,000 or more yards in an NFL season. Half of the 5,000-yard seasons in league history belong to **Drew Brees** of the New Orleans Saints. Brees threw for 5,069 yards in 2008, 5,476 yards in 2011, 5,177 yards in 2012, and 5,162 yards in 2013. No other quarterback has more than one season of 5,000 or more passing yards. The other members of the 5,000-yard club are the Miami Dolphins' Dan Marino (5,084 yards in 1984), the New England Patriots' Tom Brady (5,235 in 2011), the Detroit Lions' Matthew Stafford (5,038 in '11), and the Denver Broncos' Peyton Manning (a record 5,477 in '13).

8

SEED ADVANCING

No Number 8 seed had beaten a Number 1 seed in the NBA playoffs until Dikembe Mutombo led the Denver Nuggets to an upset of the Seattle SuperSonics in 1994. The Philadelphia 76ers became the fifth Number 8 seed ever to win a series when they beat the Chicago Bulls in 2012.

80

GOALS IN A SEASON

On March 19, 1991, Brett Hull of the St. Louis Blues scored his 80th goal of the season in a 2–1 win over the Washington Capitals. Hull joined Wayne Gretzky and Mario Lemieux as the only players ever to reach 80 goals in one season. (Gretzky did it twice for the Edmonton Oilers.) The Golden Brett would score six more goals to surpass Lemieux's 85-goal performance for the Pittsburgh Penguins in 1988–89. No player has reached 80 goals in a season since.

4

GRAND SLAMS IN FIRST AT-BAT

The bases were loaded when **Daniel Nava** of the Boston Red Sox stepped to the plate for the first time in his career. On the first pitch he saw from Philadelphia Phillies pitcher Joe Blanton, Nava hit a grand slam. Nava became only the fourth player ever to hit a grand slam his first time up in the majors.

30

RUNS SCORED BY A TEAM IN ONE GAME

In the first game of a doubleheader on August 22, 2007, the Texas Rangers turned a 3–0 deficit into a 30–3 victory over the Baltimore Orioles. The Rangers became the ninth team ever, and first team in more than 110 years, to score 30 runs in a major league game.

3,000

POINTS IN ONE SEASON

When **Michael Jordan** scored 3,041 points for the Chicago Bulls in 1986–87, it was only the fourth time in NBA history that a player scored 3,000 or more points in a season. The other three times were by Wilt Chamberlain, in 1960–61, '61–62, and '62–63.

50

ACES IN A TENNIS MATCH

An ace in tennis is a serve that wins a point without the receiving player making contact with the ball. Only 10 times has a pro player served 50 or more aces in one match. Never did it happen on a stage bigger than when Roger Federer aced Andy Roddick 50 times in the 2009 Wimbledon final. Federer's victory gave him his 15th career Major title, breaking Pete Sampras's record.

7

TOUCHDOWN PASSES IN A GAME

In a 49-20 win over the Raiders in Oakland on November 3, 2013, Philadelphia Eagles quarterback **Nick Foles** became only the seventh player in NFL history to throw seven TD passes in a game.

20 WINS IN

A ROW

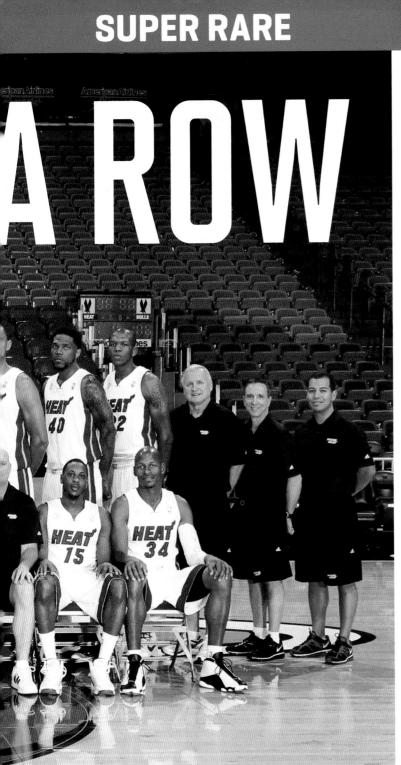

Only four teams have ever won 20 or more games in a row during an NBA regular season. The last squad to do it was the Miami Heat, who won 27 straight from February 3, 2013, through March 27.

4 STRAIGHT HOME RUNS BY A TEAM IN A GAME

Adam LaRoche, Miguel Montero, Mark Reynolds, and Stephen Drew of the Arizona Diamondbacks all homered in a row against the Milwaukee Brewers on August 11, 2010. It was the seventh time ever that major league teammates hit four straight homers.

6

COMEBACKS FROM A 3-TO-1 DEFICIT IN A WORLD SERIES

The last team to rally from a 3–1 deficit to win the World Series was the Kansas City Royals, in 1985. The Royals won Game 7 over the St. Louis Cardinals, 11–0, behind the pitching of **Bret Saberhagen**, who was named Series MVP. The Royals are one of only six teams ever to come back from a 3–1 deficit to win the World Series.

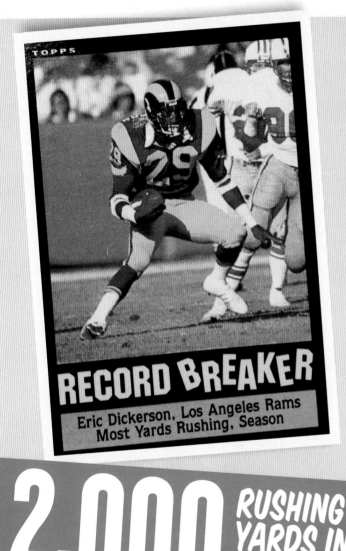

RECORD BREAKER

Eric Dickerson, Los Angeles Rams
Most Yards Rushing, Season

2,000 RUSHING YARDS IN A SEASON

★ ★ ★ ERIC DICKERSON ★ ★ ★

Only seven NFL players have rushed for 2,000 or more yards in a season. The record of 2,105 was set in 1984 by **Eric Dickerson** of the Los Angeles Rams. The closest anyone has come to Dickerson's mark was Adrian Peterson of the Minnesota Vikings, in 2012. Peterson rushed for 2,097 yards, coming up eight yards short of the record.

1,000

ASSISTS IN A SEASON

Only nine times in NBA history has a player reached 1,000 assists in a season. John Stockton of the Utah Jazz did it a remarkable seven of those nine times, including 1990–91, when he set an NBA record with 1,164. Stockton, who led the league in assists for nine straight seasons from 1987–88 to '95–96, is the NBA's all-time leader with 15,806 career assists. The only other players to reach 1,000 assists in a season are Kevin Porter (1,099 in 1978–79) and Isaiah Thomas (1,123 in '84–85), both for the Detroit Pistons.

MVP AWARDS WON BY NHL GOALIES

Only seven times has a goaltender won the Hart Trophy, which is the award given to the NHL's most valuable player. **Dominik Hasek** is the only goalie to win the Hart Trophy twice, doing so in back-to-back seasons for the Buffalo Sabres, in 1996–97 and '97–98. Nicknamed "The Dominator," Hasek earned the Vezina Trophy as the league's best goaltender six times during his 16-year NHL career.

4 ROOKIE MVPs

Only four rookies have ever earned league MVP honors in the history of major pro sports. The last time it happened was in 2001, when **Ichiro Suzuki** of the Seattle Mariners was named American League MVP after leading the league in both batting average (.350) and stolen bases (56). He became the first major league player to lead his league in both categories since Jackie Robinson in 1949. The only other major leaguer to be named MVP as a rookie was Fred Lynn of the Boston Red Sox, in 1975. The two other times the feat was accomplished in major pro sports were both in the NBA. Wilt Chamberlain was the first to do it, with the Philadelphia Warriors, in 1959–60. Wes Unseld was named MVP after his rookie season for the Baltimore Bullets, in 1968–69.

4. QUADRUPLE-DOUBLES

In his first game as a member of the Chicago Bulls, on October 18, 1974, Nate Thurmond had 22 points, 14 rebounds, 13 assists, and 12 blocked shots in a 120–115 overtime win against the Atlanta Hawks. It was the first quadruple-double in NBA history. There have been only three quadruple-doubles since: Alvin Robertson in 1986, Hakeem Olajuwon in 1990, and David Robinson in 1994.

7

FIELD GOALS IN A GAME

Only six times has a kicker made seven or more field goals in an NFL game. The only player to kick eight is **Rob Bironas** of the Tennessee Titans, in a 38–36 win over the Houston Texans on October 21, 2007.

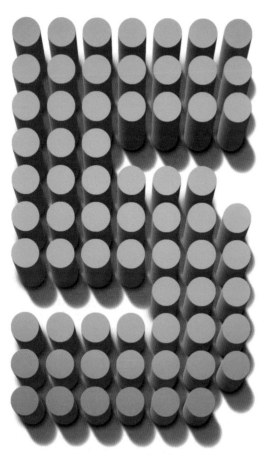

COMEBACKS FROM A 3-TO-0 SERIES DEFICIT IN ANY SPORT

Four of the five times a major pro sports team has come back from a 3–0 deficit to win a best-of-seven series have been in the NHL. The only other time was in baseball, when the New York Yankees got within three outs of sweeping the **Boston Red Sox** in the 2004 American League Championship Series. David Ortiz (Number 34) hit a two-run walk-off home run to right field in the 12th inning of Game 4. Ortiz then came through with an RBI single in the 14th inning of Game 5. The Sox completed the comeback with back-to-back wins in New York in Games 6 and 7.

In a 2013 victory over the Dallas Cowboys, Calvin Johnson of the Detroit Lions became only the third NFL player ever to gain 300 or more receiving yards in a game.

ALMOST IMPOSSIBLE

2

NATIONAL CHAMPS FROM ONE SCHOOL IN THE SAME SEASON

Only twice have the men's and women's teams from the same college won the NCAA Division I basketball championship in the same season — both times it was the University of Connecticut Huskies. UConn accomplished the feat first in 2004. In 2014, **Shabazz Napier** scored 22 points in UConn's title game win over Kentucky. One night later, **Breanna Stewart** scored 21 in the women's win over Notre Dame.

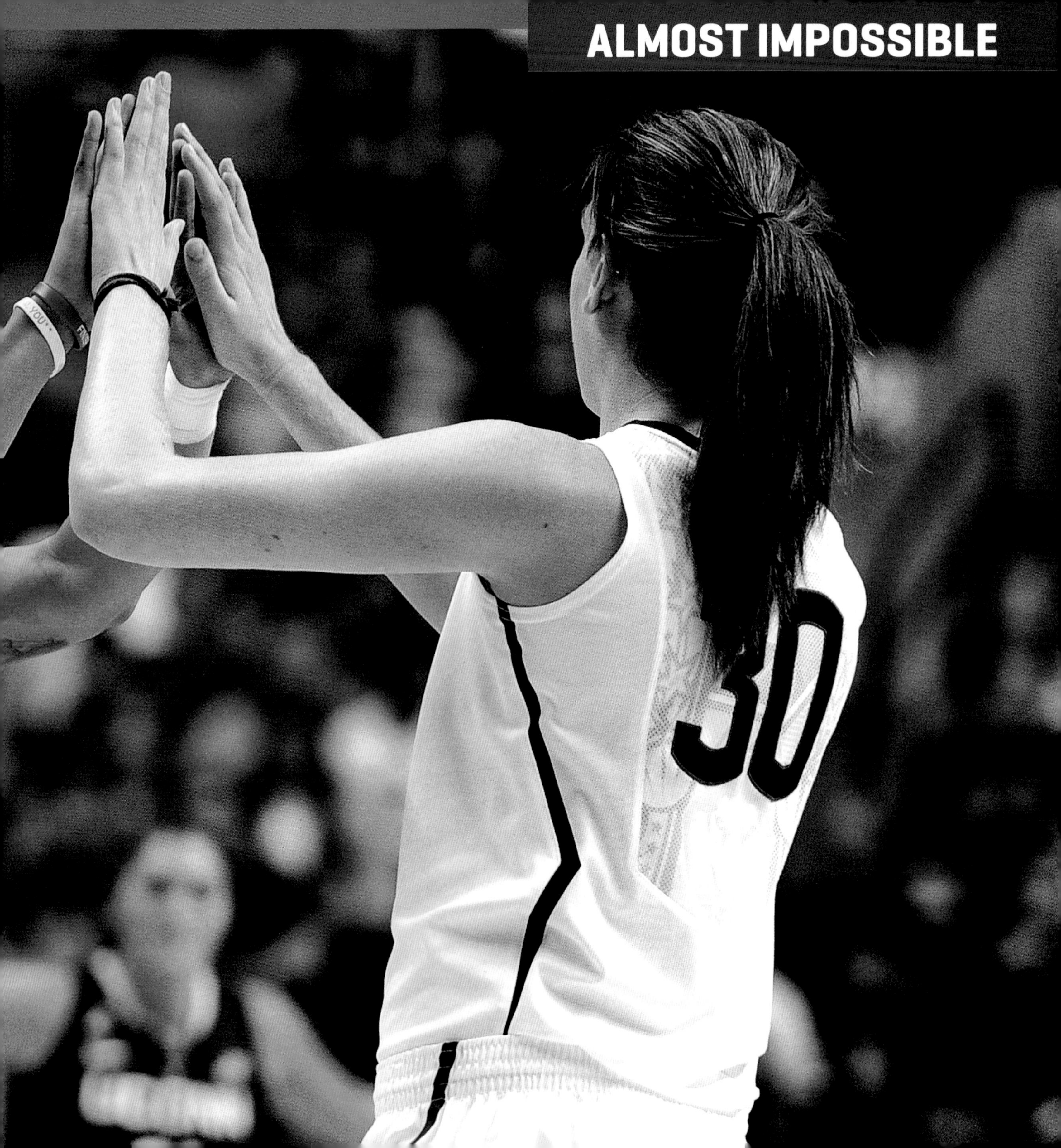
30

20
STRIKEOUTS IN A GAME

There have been only three times that a major league pitcher has struck out 20 batters in a nine-inning game. **Roger Clemens** did it twice for the Boston Red Sox, against the Seattle Mariners in 1986, and against the Detroit Tigers in 1996. Kerry Wood of the Chicago Cubs struck out 20 Houston Astros in a 1998 game.

5 GOALS IN A WORLD CUP GAME

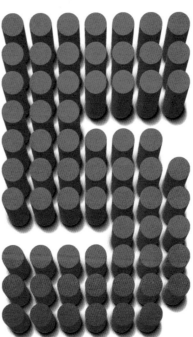

Michelle Akers of the United States scored five goals against Taiwan at the 1991 Women's World Cup. Russia's Oleg Salenko matched Akers's mark at the 1994 men's World Cup.

SHORT-HANDED HAT TRICK

Theo Fleury was best known for how aggressively he played hockey despite the fact that he was only 5' 6". But he was a very talented offensive player, too. On March 9, 1991, Fleury scored three short-handed goals in the Calgary Flames' 8–4 win over the St. Louis Blues. He scored his first goal with the Blues on a power play less than six minutes into the first period. Fleury scored again that way during the first minute of the third period, and for a third time with only 2:25 remaining in the game. It's the first and last time that an NHL player scored three short-handed goals in the same game.

2

NO-HITTERS ON THE SAME DAY

Less than an hour before the Los Angeles Dodgers faced the St. Louis Cardinals on June 29, 1990, Fernando Valenzuela saw on a TV in the clubhouse that Dave Stewart of the Oakland A's had pitched a no-hitter against the Toronto Blue Jays. "Now maybe we'll see another no-hitter," Valenzuela said to his teammates. Sure enough, Valuenzuela no-hit the Cardinals. It was the first time in more than 92 years that two no-hitters were thrown on the same day.

ERNIE NEVERS
(Stanford)
6-1, 205
Fullback
Duluth Eskimos, Chicago Cardinals
1926-1931

The Immortal Roll

USED WITH PERMISSION OF PRO FOOTBALL HALL OF FAME

6 RUSHING TOUCHDOWNS IN ONE GAME

★ ★ ★ ERNIE NEVERS ★ ★ ★

Ernie Nevers scored all 40 of the Chicago Cardinals' points in his team's 40–6 victory over the Chicago Bears on November 28, 1929. He did it by rushing for six touchdowns and kicking four extra points. Nevers remains the only player ever to rush for six touchdowns in a single NFL game. It's the longest-standing record in league history.

100

PLUS/MINUS RATING

Only two NHL players have ever had a plus/minus rating of 100 or better in a season. The first to do it was Bobby Orr of the Boston Bruins, who had a plus-124 rating in 1970–71. The only player to do it since then was the Montreal Canadiens' Larry Robinson, in 1976–77. Robinson had a plus-120 to help the Canadiens win the 20th Stanley Cup in franchise history.

COLLEGE BASKETBALL QUADRUPLE-DOUBLE

On November 13, 2007, 6' 3" guard **Lester Hudson** had 25 points, 12 rebounds, 10 assists, and 10 steals in the University of Tennessee-Martin's 116–74 victory over Central Baptist College. Hudson became the first player in Division I men's college basketball history to record a quadruple-double. He was disappointed that the feat got only a brief mention on ESPN's *SportsCenter*. After all, "Michael Jordan and Magic Johnson never did it," Hudson said.

3

SHORT-HANDED GOALS ON ONE PENALTY

The game between the Boston Bruins and Carolina Hurricanes was scoreless on April 10, 2010, when Boston's Matt Hunwick was called for a hooking penalty with 18 seconds left in the first period. When the teams came out for the second period with the Hurricanes still on the power play, Daniel Paille, **Blake Wheeler**, and Steve Begin all scored within the first 1 minute and 36 seconds. The Bruins are the only team to score three short-handed goals on the same penalty.

100 POINTS IN ONE NBA GAME

Star center **Wilt Chamberlain** of the Philadelphia Warriors had 41 points at halftime, 69 after three quarters, and 75 with 10 minutes left in a game against the New York Knicks on March 2, 1962. With 46 seconds left, Chamberlain finished off a lob pass to reach 100 points, the most ever in an NBA game. It's a record that still stands and quite possibly will never be broken.

30

ASSISTS IN A GAME

Scott Skiles was known for his excellent court vision during a 10-year NBA career as a point guard with the Milwaukee Bucks, Indiana Pacers, Orlando Magic, Washington Bullets, and Philadelphia 76ers. On December 30, 1990, he set the record for most assists in a game with 30 in the Magic's 155–116 win over the Denver Nuggets. It's a record that still stands

2 HOLES-IN-ONE IN ONE PGA TOUR ROUND

Yusaku Miyazato became the second golfer to make two holes-in-one in the same round of a PGA Tour tournament when he did it during the second round of the 2006 Reno-Tahoe Open. Miyazato's first hole-in-one came when he hit a 4-iron on the 230-yard seventh hole. The second one came on the 173-yard 12th hole. He joined Bill Whedon (1955), Jack Rule (1964), Glen Day (1994), and Bob Tway (1994), as the only players in PGA Tour history to record two holes-in-one in an event. Miyazato and Whedon are the only golfers to do it in the same round.

300

RECEIVING YARDS IN A GAME

In a game against the Dallas Cowboys on October 27, 2013, **Calvin Johnson** of the Detroit Lions became only the third player ever to reach 300 receiving yards in a game. Johnson's 329 receiving yards was the second-highest total in NFL history. (Flipper Anderson's 336 receiving yards for the Los Angeles Rams on November 26, 1989, is the NFL record.) Johnson's most important yards were the 22 he gained on a catch in the final minute to set the Lions up at the Dallas 1-yard line. From there, Detroit quarterback Matthew Stafford plunged the ball into the end zone with 12 seconds left to give the Lions a dramatic 31–30 victory.

10

POINTS IN A GAME

The greatest single-game performance in NHL history happened on February 7, 1976. That's when Darryl Sittler of the Toronto Maple Leafs recorded six goals and four assists in an 11–4 win over the Boston Bruins. Sittler remains the only NHL player to reach 10 points in a game — no other player has reached even nine points in a game. "I'm proud to hold the record," Sittler said recently. When asked if he thought it would ever be broken, Sittler said, "It's a longshot. There are very few times when 10 goals are scored by one team, let alone for one player to be in on all 10."

20

CATCHES IN A GAME

Only two players have caught 20 or more passes in an NFL game. The first was Terrell Owens, who hauled in 20 for the San Francisco 49ers against the Chicago Bears on December 17, 2000. Brandon Marshall broke Owens's record with 21 catches for the Denver Broncos against the Indianapolis Colts on December 13, 2009. Broncos quarterback Kyle Orton targeted Marshall 28 times in the game.

2

CYCLES IN THE SAME MONTH

Aaron Hill of the Arizona Diamondbacks hit for the cycle on June 18, 2012, and then again on June 29. He became the second player to hit for the cycle twice in the same month, and the first to do it since 1883.

2
PERFECT
SETS

Yaroslava Shvedova of Kazakhstan won 24 straight points in a 6–0, 6–4 victory over Italy's Sara Errani in the third round of Wimbledon in 2012. It was the first time since 1968, the year the Open era began, that a player played a set perfectly at a Grand Slam event. The only other perfect set since the Open era began was at the 1983 WCT Gold Coast Classic. That's when when Bill Scanlon won all 24 points in the second set of a first-round victory over Marcos Hocevar.

1 FRESHMAN SCORING CHAMPION

When Jason Conley averaged 29.3 points per game for the Virginia Military Institute (VMI) Keydets in 2001–02, he became the first NCAA Division I freshman ever to lead men's college basketball in scoring. Conley would go on to begin his sophomore season at VMI before transferring to the University of Missouri.

70
WINS IN A SEASON

With superstar Michael Jordan leading the way, the 1995–96 **Chicago Bulls** became the first NBA team to win 70 games in a season. (The previous record was 69, held by the 1971-72 Los Angeles Lakers.) The Bulls opened the season by going 41–3 over their first 44 games. They ended up leading the NBA in offensive and defensive efficiency, and they outscored their opponents by an average of 12.2 points per game. Chicago didn't let up in the playoffs, either, winning 15 of 18 postseason games. The Bulls beat the Seattle SuperSonics in the NBA Finals in six games to win their fourth title in six years.

90

GOALS IN A SEASON

When **Wayne Gretzky** of the Edmonton Oilers scored 92 goals in 1981–82, he crushed the previous record of 76 that was set by Phil Esposito of the Boston Bruins in 1970–71. Gretzky got off to a hot start, scoring 50 goals in his first 39 games. He notched the record-breaker on February 24, 1982, in a game against the Buffalo Sabres. No other player has ever reached 90 goals in an NHL season.

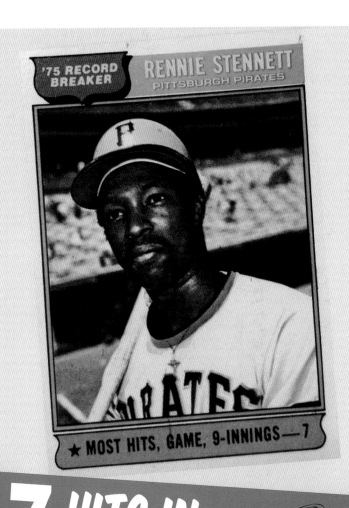

'75 RECORD BREAKER

RENNIE STENNETT
PITTSBURGH PIRATES

★ MOST HITS, GAME, 9-INNINGS — 7

7 HITS IN ONE GAME

★ ★ ★ RENNIE STENNETT ★ ★ ★

Pittsburgh Pirates second baseman **Rennie Stennett** collected a hit in all seven of his at-bats during a 22–0 victory over the Chicago Cubs on September 16, 1975. Stennett became only the second player in Major League Baseball history — and the first player in more than 83 years — to collect seven hits in a nine-inning game.

5 TD RECEPTIONS IN A GAME

When Jerry Rice of the San Francisco 49ers caught five touchdown passes in a 45–35 win over the Atlanta Falcons on October 14, 1990, he became the first wide receiver ever to do so. The only other two players to catch five TD passes in a game were tight ends: Bob Shaw of the Chicago Cardinals against the Baltimore Colts in 1950, and the San Diego Chargers' Kellen Winslow against the Oakland Raiders in 1981.

1 UNDEFEATED SEASON IN NFL HISTORY

Led by head coach Don Shula, the Miami Dolphins had the NFL's top-ranked offense and top-ranked defense in 1972. Those units led the team to a 17–0 record, which is the only undefeated season in league history. It was Shula's run-heavy offense that led to Larry Csonka and Mercury Morris becoming the first teammates to each run for 1,000 yards in the same season. The Dolphins capped their perfect season with a 14–7 win over the Washington Redskins in Super Bowl VII.

100 POINTS IN A HALF BY A TEAM

Only once in NBA history has a team scored 100 or more points in a half. It happened on November 10, 1990, when the Phoenix Suns scored 107 points in the first half of a game against the Denver Nuggets. Suns point guard Kevin Johnson scored 23 points and led Phoenix with 17 assists. The Suns went on to win, 173–143. The 316 total points is tied for the sixth-most ever in an NBA game.

BONUS!
IT'S NEVER HAPPENED!

TURN TO FIND OUT! →

300

RUSHING YARDS IN A GAME

No player has ever rushed for 300 yards in an NFL game. The running back who came the closest was **Adrian Peterson** of the Minnesota Vikings. In only the eighth game of his rookie season, on November 4, 2007, Peterson set the NFL's single-game rushing record with 296 yards in a 35–17 victory over the San Diego Chargers. Peterson broke the mark that was set on September 14, 2003, when the Baltimore Ravens' Jamal Lewis rushed for 295 yards in a 33–13 win over the Cleveland Browns. "I was out playing ball," Peterson said after his record-setting performance. "I wasn't thinking about the record at all."

50

GOALS BY AN NHL DEFENSEMAN

No NHL defenseman has come as close to scoring 50 goals in a season as the Edmonton Oilers' **Paul Coffey** in 1985–86. His 48 goals that season are the most ever by an NHL defenseman.

0
HOME LOSSES IN A SEASON

The **Boston Celtics** almost became the first NBA team to go unbeaten at home when they went 50–1 in 1985–86.

2,000
RECEIVING YARDS IN A SEASON

No player has ever reached 2,000 receiving yards in an NFL season. Cleveland Browns receiver **Josh Gordon** led the NFL with 1,646 receiving yards in 2013 despite the fact that he missed the first two games of the season. Gordon became the first player to surpass 200 receiving yards in back-to-back regular season games. He had 237 yards against the Pittsburgh Steelers in Week 12, and 261 receiving yards against the Jacksonville Jaguars in Week 13.

70

DOUBLES IN A SEASON

No major league player has ever hit 70 doubles in a season, and only six players have reached even 60. When Todd Helton of the Colorado Rockies led the majors with 59 doubles in 2000, he nearly became the first player since 1936 to reach 60 doubles in a season. Helton's 2000 season was one of the best ever for a hitter. In addition to leading the majors in doubles, he won the National League batting title with a .372 average. His 147 RBIs also led the majors, and he hit 42 home runs. Helton spent his entire 17-year career with the Rockies before retiring after the 2013 season.

100

FREE THROWS IN A ROW

No NBA player has ever made 100 straight free throws. The one who came closest was Micheal Williams, who made 97 straight for the Minnesota Timberwolves. Williams's streak began on March 24, 1993, and didn't end until he missed on November 9.

40

WINS IN A SEASON

The 2011–12 University of Kentucky Wildcats came within two victories of becoming the first NCAA Division I men's basketball team to win 40 in a season. Kentucky went 38–2 and were led to the national championship by Anthony Davis, who won the Naismith Trophy for men's college player of the year.

5

INTERCEPTIONS IN AN NFL GAME

A total of 19 players have intercepted four passes in an NFL game, but nobody has ever picked off five. The last player with four picks in a game was DeAngelo Hall of the Washington Redskins against the Chicago Bears on October 24, 2010. He returned one of those picks 92 yards for a touchdown for the final score of the day in the Redskins' 17–14 victory.

200 POINTS IN AN NBA GAME

No NBA team has ever scored 200 points in a game. The two teams that came the closest were the Detroit Pistons and Denver Nuggets — in the same game! The Pistons won in triple-overtime, 186–184, on December 13, 1983. Star point guard Isiah Thomas led Detroit with 47 points and 17 assists. The Nuggets were led by Kiki Vandeweghe's 51 points and 47 from Alex English.

20 TOTAL BASES IN A GAME

No major league player has come closer to reaching 20 total bases in a game than Shawn Green did for the Los Angeles Dodgers on May 23, 2002. Green set a record with 19 total bases against the Milwaukee Brewers when he hit four home runs to go along with a double and a single.

INDEX

BASEBALL

BASKETBALL

Smith, J.R. **60**

Stewart, Breanna **93**

Stockton, John **83**

Thomas, Isiah **125**

Thurmond, Nate **86**

Williams, Micheal **121**

Wooden, John **55**

BOWLING

Sonnenfeld, Jeremy **41**

FOOTBALL

Bironas, Rob **86**

Bledsoe, Drew **42**

Brady, Tom **29**

Brees, Drew **72**

Cruz, Victor **40**

Denver Broncos **44**

Dickerson, Eric **83**

Foles, Nick **79**

Gordon, Josh **119**

Hall, DeAngelo **124**

Harrison, James **14**

Johnson, Calvin **104**

Manning, Peyton **10**

Marshall, Brandon **106**

Nevers, Ernie **97**

New Orleans Saints **50**

Peterson, Adrian **116**

Rice, Jerry **113**

Romo, Tony **36**

Shula, Don **114**

Tomlinson, LaDainian **22**

Washington, Leon **66**

Wilson, Russell **56**

GOLF

Miyazato, Yusaku **103**

Oosthuizen, Louis **53**

Sorenstam, Annika **66**

HOCKEY

Boston Bruins **100**

Brodeur, Martin **49**

Coffey, Paul **118**

Fleury, Theo **95**

Gretzky, Wayne **113**

Halak, Jaroslav **58**

Hasek, Dominik **84**

Hull, Brett **74**

Kerr, Tim **32**

Mogilny, Alexander **42**

Orr, Bobby **47**

Quick, Jonathan **30**

Robinson, Larry **97**

Sittler, Darryl **106**

Stamkos, Steven **25**

Varlamov, Semyon **18**

SOCCER

Akers, Michelle **95**

TENNIS

Agassi, Andre **71**

Federer, Roger **78**

Shvedova, Yaroslava **108**

PHOTO CREDITS

TITLE PAGE
Chris Graythen/Getty Images

TABLE OF CONTENTS
Kevin C. Cox/Getty Images

RARE (PAGES 6–33)
Al Bello/Getty Images (Harrison); Lenny Ignelzi/AP (Davis); Dustin Bradford/Getty Images (Manning); Topps Company (DiMaggio); Focus On Sport/Getty Images (Johnson); Leon Halip/Getty Images (Sanchez); Jon Blacker/AP (Encarnacion); Mark Humphrey/AP (Harrison); Lynne Sladky/AP (James); Michael Zagaris/Getty Images (Trout); Bill Baptist/Getty Images (Eaton); Jim McIsaac/Getty Images (Delabar); Tony Gutierrez/AP (Varlamov); Mark Duncan/AP (Profar); Rob Tringali/Sportschrome/Getty Images (Tomlinson); David Durochik/AP (Rios); Ben Margot/AP (Allen); Elaine Thompson/AP (Marte); Chris Szagola/Getty Images (Stamkos); Matt Slocum/AP (Phillies); Matt Slocum/AP (Phillies); Imperial Tobacco Company (Malone); Getty Images (Ryan); Elsa Garrison/Getty Images (Brady); Josh Thompson/AP (Quick); Denis Brodeur/Getty Images (Kerr); Matt York/AP (Johnson)

REALLY RARE (PAGES 34–61)
Leon Halip/Getty Images (Cabrera); Wesley Hitt/Getty Images (Romo); Chris Carlson/AP (Anderson); Nathaniel S. Butler/Getty Images (Miller/Rose); Christopher Pasatieri/Getty Images (Cruz); Topps Company (Lazzeri); Courtesy Sport Bowl/Sioux Falls, S.D. (Sonnenfeld); Mitchell Layton/Getty Images (Mogilny); Brian Drake/Getty Images (Robertson); Ronald Martinez/Getty Images (Thomas); Phil Sears/Getty Images (Laettner); Charlie Riedel/AP (Cabrera); Bruce Bennett/Getty Images (Orr); Kidwiler Collection/Getty Images (Larsen); Elsa Garrison/Getty Images (Brodeur); Aaron M. Sprecher/AP (Colston); Tom Gannam/AP (Tatis); Focus On Sport/Getty Images (Bledsoe); The Sporting News Publishing Company/Getty Images (Wambsganss); Streeter Lecka/Getty Images (Oosthuizen); Streeter Lecka/Getty Images (Oosthuizen); Winslow Townson/AP (Buchholz); AP Images (Wooden); Otto Greule Jr./Getty Images (Wilson); Gerry Broome/AP (Halak); Collegiate Images/Getty Images (Maravich); Bill Chan/AP (Griffey Jr.); Nathaniel S. Butler/Getty Images (Smith)

SUPER RARE (PAGES 62–89)
Nathaniel S. Butler/Getty Images (Jordan); Elaine Thompson/AP (Mariners); Mike Fiala/AP (Sorenstam);

Kevin Terrell/AP (Washington); Michael Spomer/AP (McDermott); Matt York/AP (Nash); Al Behrman/AP (Brickman); Fleer Corporation (Canseco); Michel Euler/AP (Agassi); Rusty Costanza/AP (Brees); Gary Stewart/AP (Mutombo); Denis Brodeur/Getty Images (Hull); Michael Ivins/Boston Red Sox/Getty Images (Nava); Lloyd Fox/AP (Rangers); Andrew D. Bernstein/Getty Images (Jordan); Julian Finney/Getty Images (Federer); Greg Trott/AP (Foles); Issac Baldizon/Getty Images (Heat); Jim Prisching/Getty Images (Drew); Focus on Sport/Getty Images (Saberhagen); Focus on Sport/Getty Images (Saberhagen); Topps Company (Dickerson); Rich Pedroncelli/AP (Stockton); Jim Leary/Getty Images (Hasek); Elaine Thompson/AP (Ichiro); Dick Raphael/Getty Images (Thurmond); Kevin C. Cox/Getty Images (Bironas); Al Bello/Getty Images (Red Sox)

ALMOST IMPOSSIBLE (PAGES 90–114)
Duane Burleson/AP (Johnson); Jessica Hill/AP (Napier/Stewart); Tim Fitzgerald/AP (Clemens); Chen Guo/AP (Akers); Brian Winkler/Getty Images (Fleury); NBA Photos/Getty Images (Bulls); Focus On Sport/Getty Images (Stewart); Focus On Sport/Getty Images (Valenzuela); Fleer Corporation (Nevers); Steve Babineau/Getty Images (Robinson, Wheeler); Paul Vathis/AP

(Chamberlain); Nathaniel S. Butler/Getty Images (Skiles); Tim Dunn/AP (Miyazato); Leon Halip/Getty Images (Johnson); Steve Babineau/Getty Images (Sittler); Darron Cummings/AP (Marshall); Lisa Blumenfeld/Getty Images (Hill); EMPICS Sport/AP (Shvedova); Joe Cavaretta/AP (Conley); Joe Cavaretta/AP (Conley); Wade Payne/AP (Hudson); DK Photo/Allsport USA/Getty Images (Gretzky); Topps Company (Stennett); Stephen Dunn/Getty Images (Rice); AP (Shula); Andrew D. Bernstein/Getty Images (Johnson)

NEVER HAPPENED (PAGES 116–125)
Duane Burleson/AP (Johnson); Tom Dahlin/Getty Images (Peterson); Bruce Bennett/Getty Images (Coffey); Dick Raphael/Getty Images (Celtics); David Richard/AP (Gordon); Briah Bahr/Getty Images (Helton); Dale Tait/Getty Images (Williams); Andy Lyons/Getty Images (Davis); The Washington Post/Getty Images (Hall); AP Images (Thomas); Jim Rogash/Getty Images (Green)

BACK COVER
Al Pereira/Getty Images (Manning); Al Bello/Getty Images (Sanchez); Dick Raphael/Getty Images (Chamberlain); Bruce Bennett/Getty Images (Gretzky)